AWAKEN
THE
BEAR

BY BRIAN MEIER

The chapters that follow lay out simple, actionable skills that you can foster in yourself and encourage in others. The goal is to reorient your inner compass towards your essential wildness, a pattern of being that many of us have partly forgotten or suppressed. The primary aim of this guide is to explore practical ways that we can return to this pattern and summon a deeper, wilder, and more authentic way of being.

TABLE OF CONTENTS

INTRO

THE BEAR STIRS

I

WILD AS THE WIND

A WILDNESS OF BEING

THE TAMING OF THE YOU

II

FIND YOUR TRAIL

ANOTHER WAY TO PAY ATTENTION

MIND LIKE WATER

III

MORE SOUND, LESS NOISE

FAST TWITCH ANIMALS

ABORIGINAL SENSIBLE MUCHNESS

CODA

THE BEAR AWAKENS

THE BEAR STIRS

The seed for this book was planted many years ago when I was young and single and driving across the interior of Alaska in a borrowed Pontiac.

For two weeks, I camped and fished in a meandering route, never traveling for more than a few hours without stopping to cast for trout, or to hike, or to watch a salmon wheel spin. I didn't know then that a solo drive across Alaska was a luxury of youth and good fortune. I didn't understand how two weeks on the road and in the woods could change me.

Twenty years have passed since that summer, but there are still memories from that trip that return to me with granular precision. I can recall, for instance, a morning hike in the rain, the redolent smell of earth and pine, my heart thrumming when a bear emerged suddenly from the brush, steam rising from its fur. I can still hear the sonorous heaving of its breath. I can still feel the fear that froze me in place.

Time collapsed as I locked eyes with that bear. My mind went quiet.[1] There was a slowing, an underwater stillness. The landscape felt primordial. The air, otherworldly.

When I began writing this book and thinking about the idea of "wild"—both as a place and as a way of being—my mind returned to that bear: The way he lumbered into my world, the way his eyes spoke meaning, the way he vanished into a stand of birch and became memory. That bear now feels archetypal, like a character in a parable or a myth. I cannot think of Alaska without also thinking of that bear's wild presence. How necessary he seems, how consonant. For me, that bear is now equal parts flesh and symbol—real, in as much as memory can be real, but also emblematic.

"Time collapsed as I locked eyes with that bear. My mind went quiet. There was a slowing, an underwater stillness. The landscape felt primordial. The air, otherworldly."

The goal of this book is to explore a wilder way of being. In the following pages I will first present the bear as an idea anchored in our subconscious—that we were once wild and there is a resonant past that still speaks to us if we listen.

Next, I will use the bear as a stepping off point for a broader discussion about wild landscapes and how they affect us.

Finally, and most importantly, I will synthesize the ideas of landscape and resonant past into a series of invitations: I want you to compare yourself to that bear. I want you to think about its freedom to roam and the landscape that it calls home. I want you to see its strength and vitality. Then I want you to consider the possibility that its power and its freedoms are yours too. That they are your birthright. That there is a wildness within you that awaits an awakening.

CHAPTER 1

WILD AS THE WIND

"You didn't come into this world. You came out of it, like a
wave from the ocean. You are not a stranger here."
—*Alan Watts*

I was at home in Spokane writing, my dog at my feet. Outside, the snow had turned to rain. What was white was now mottled with wet earth. The roads, black-iced.

Words came slowly. Sentences trailed off. My mind felt as dull as the weather. So I leashed my dog, Basho, a Red Heeler named after the Japanese poet who loved walking.

We followed a side street for half a mile through my neighborhood past houses and parked cars. A man shoveled ice off his steps. A cat watched us from a windowsill. The sound of wet tires on asphalt. Wood smoke in the air.

After ten minutes, we arrived at Manito park,[2] a sprawling greenspace near my home. The pond at the entrance to the park was frozen but slick with rain. There were skate marks on the ice—white scratches on black like chalk on slate. Were some of the marks mine? I had skated here with my youngest son the night before—my wife watching from the bench, Basho at her feet, his ears back, unsure of the winter ice.

Beyond the pond, there was a patch of snow on the shaded north of the hill. Basho pulled me towards it, taunted by a squirrel. We marked our passage across the snow with footprints and crossed others. I saw turkey tracks, raccoon tracks, and the paw prints of a another dog, or maybe a coyote.

An airplane crossed overhead. I heard cars passing on the nearby road. But the animal tracks told another story, one that was wilder and untamed.

We followed the raccoon tracks up the hill. At the summit, patches of grass broke through the snow. To the south, a jogger circled the pond. To the north, just barely visible over the trees, the city. A white haze over the river.

Basho and I had often climbed this hill on our walks. We both know it well. I have wondered more than once how it was that it escaped the park's manicured landscaping and bordered paths and gazebos. Was it too precipitous, too rocky for construction? Or, perhaps, was it possible that someone long ago felt a wild resonance on this hill that seemed worth saving?

Less than a century ago, the entire park was undeveloped, wooded. The only paths were game trails. There were elk and moose and maybe black bear. Now, in summer, there are picnics and Frisbees and strollers. A restaurant sells sandwiches and ice cream. On most winter days there is sledding and cross-country skiing, and in autumn, young parents take photos of their kids at play in the fallen leaves.

But on this day, the day of our walk, the low-slung clouds and cold had emptied the park. The solitude made it easy to imagine the park as a wilder place—to feel an ancient presence rising from the earth and silence.

"The solitude made it easy to imagine the park as a wilder place—to feel an ancient presence rising from the earth and silence."

An afternoon walk, a quiet hill, and there I was, whispering to ghosts a hundred thousand years old. Then a car horn sounds in the distance and the moment is gone.

The point is simple but important: The wild can still sometimes be stirred within us. It remains in our memory banks and can be conjured by a smell, a touch, or even a simple moment of solitude.

We depend on the past to interpret the present. It offers a lineage, a continuity, and a security. Wild places render the present recognizable, remind us of a shared history between ourselves and tree and stone.

To believe that certain places resonate on a wilder frequency, a frequency that teaches us who we are, is not indulging in myth or magical thinking. For centuries, the wisest among us—Schopenhauer, Kant, Nietzsche, Wordsworth, Thoreau, to name a few—all in their own way came to a similar conclusion: There is a raw wildness in us, an animal nature, that needs to be recovered, understood, and animated.

"There is a raw wildness in us, an animal nature, that needs to be recovered, understood, and animated."

There are people, a small minority, who feel this truth so strongly that it leads them to an alternate life. They immerse themselves in the wild and commune with this resonance. We know their stories well. Some of us admire them. Some of us think them fools.

For most of us, however, the importance of the wild is not so much as a place of permanent escape. The true importance of the wild is that when we open ourselves to it, it puts us in touch with something greater. It teaches us how to live better in the everyday and ordinary.

--

Basho tugged on his leash and barked impatiently. A crow circled then landed nearby. The rain began anew. My thoughts yielded again to the present, my work, my desk waiting at home, and slowly, finally, we began our return by descending the ancient hill, retracing our path, and following the melting footprints home.

A WILDNESS OF BEING

"We must become beasts to become wise."
—*Montaigne*

For children, there is no clear line between the wild and human world. Colorful animals hang from mobiles above infants' cribs. Story books are filled with friendly beasts. Stuffed bears sit next to children's pillows. Few children grow up on farms, yet we still teach them the sounds of farm animals. The word "nature" itself is derived from the Latin word for birth, suggesting, crucially, that the wild, in our culture and our psychology, is intricately linked with our beginnings.

The wild is a formative component in a child's earliest worldview. In Genesis, Adam names the animals and Eve knows their language. Animals are the conduit for Aesop's morals. In Ovid's tales, humans metamorphosize into trees and beasts. The Merry Men hide in Sherwood Forest. Peter Pan flies to Neverland. Errant knights wander in trackless woods.

But as our children mature, we pull a bizarre bait-and-switch. We let them begin life with animals roaming and prancing across the wild of their imagination, and then we gradually ween them off this narrative, telling them, with subtle and not so subtle cues that, no, in truth, that's not the way it is. It is not like that at all. And we introduce them to another story.

Like Mowgli, our children must say goodbye to the jungle and the beloved bear and move into the world of civilization and man. The nature narrative is lumped together with Santa Claus and the Tooth Fairy, relegated to white lie until the fibers unravel, the linkages break, and our children become like amnesiacs. Their place in the landscape[3] shifts:

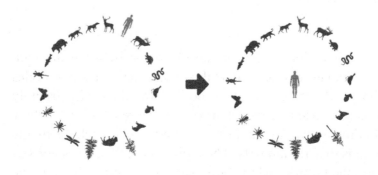

And yet all is not lost, not quite. The story of our wilder selves still echoes in our subconscious like the whisper of a ghost.[4] Dormant, but not forgotten.

All of us have gazed out a window and longed for an escape. This longing is a ghost speaking, a hunger we need to attend to. Our desktop screensavers—the picturesque beach, the iconic moon above Yosemite Valley—are yet more ghosts. We are drawn to these landscapes because they speak to something deep within us. They remind us where we are meant to be. The uncanniness of these whispers can be traced back to our earlier selves. They are an aspect of our subconscious that aches to be wild once again.

"The story of our wilder selves still echoes in our subconscious like the whisper of a ghost."

But how do we return? Over the last few decades, we've disconnected from the wild like never before. Hunting and fishing licenses,[5] national park attendance,[6] and other indicators of nature recreation have been steadily waning. American adults spend over ninety percent of their lives inside vehicles or buildings,[7] and the average American child spends fewer than thirty minutes outside per day.[8] We live now in what writer Richard Louv calls "protective house arrest."[9]

AWAKEN YOUR INNER BEAR

Live the Free Air Life: Words, in many ways, shape how people think. The Japanese word *kachou fuugetsu* literally means "flower bird wind moon," but it's commonly translated as "learn about yourself by experiencing nature." The Koreans have a similar expression, *shin to bul ee,* which means "body and soil are one." But the most well-known nature-centric expression is probably Norway's *friluftsliv*, which means "free air life." Add these three words to your lexicon and what will it mean? Perhaps, a life with more nature, more hands-off parenting, more outdoor recreation, and more play.

Get Dirty: Studies continually confirm that the microbiota that we encounter in nature is beneficial.[10] This is particularly true with children. Our modern obsession with cleanliness may be doing more harm than good. As it turns out, that dad who tells his scraped-up kid to "just throw some dirt on it" might be on to something. Should we stop washing our hands? No, of course not. That's not the point. But splashing around in a few more puddles might do us some good.

Enjoy More Dog Days: Animal lovers have long known that pets make us feel better. Science is now beginning to back this up. Dogs, studies have found, are particularly health-giving: Dog owners have fewer heart attacks,[11] and petting a dog boosts the immune system[12] while reducing stress.[13] Thinking about getting a dog? Now you have one more reason.

The empirical evidence and our intuitive awareness deliver a shared message—nature is good for us. We know that forests improve our mood. We know that spending time in the outdoors calms us. We know that people are happier, more creative, and less stressed when they have access to green spaces. We need to align what we know with how we behave.

Where we come from and what we are built for is still hard-wired within us, but the tonic of nature will remain at arm's length if we are not attentive and proactive. We must teach our children and remind ourselves that nature is neither myth nor abstraction. It's in our backyards, and parks, and gardens. It needs to be touched, though, to be activated. It needs to be heard, to be understood. The "ghosts" of our past will not return uninvited. The challenge for all of us is to become a conscious participant in its unfolding.

THE TAMING OF THE YOU

*"Even a brief glimpse of what we were is valuable to help
understand what we are."*
—Dervla Murphy

I am domesticated and you are too. Domestication is one of the legacies of human evolution.

It began around five million years ago with our first bipedal steps, increased when we began foraging and hunting in organized bands, but it was agriculture and communal living—more than anything else—that eventually tamed us.

Scientists increasingly agree that over the course of human evolution, our ancestors became less aggressive and more collaborative because of pressures to co-exist. In other words, they self-selected among themselves for a certain amount of tameness. Gradually, over thousands of years our behavior mellowed and our diet evolved. Our looks changed too: Our primitive faces became smoother and less elongated, our heads and pelvises shrank slightly, and our jaws rounded.[14]

For the most part, our self-imposed "taming" has served our species well. Despite being slow, furless, and relatively frail, domestic living freed us from the constraints of nature, which in turn set the stage for our modern ascendency from hunter to farmer to iPhone wielding urbanite. We've eradicated small pox and polio.

We've circumnavigated the globe and landed on the moon. We've conjured democracy and art and poetry from the boundless depths of our imaginations.

Many point out that this is how it should be, that life is better now, far better, and infinitely easier.

Others say, hold on, who's to say things are better? Are we healthier? Do we live longer? And where's the proof?[15]

I suggest a third viewpoint, not exactly a middle road, per say, but rather a different kind of imaginative exercise.

The question should not be whether the past was somehow better than the present or vice versa. The better question is the one that pursues windows of opportunity to become our best selves. To this end, consider the following questions:

Have we become duller, chubbier, and more docile versions of our once wild selves? When animals are domesticated they look and behave very differently from their feral ancestors. Wolves turn into dogs. Jackrabbits turn into bunny rabbits. Boars turn into pudgy pigs. Is this our story too?

Have our shelters turned against us? Finding shelter is a basic human need, but studies suggest that too much time indoors plays havoc with our circadian rhythms, which in turn fuels insomnia and anxiety.[16]

What happens when everything around us is devised to minimize physical movement, not encourage it? As we've shifted indoors, we've stopped moving. We sit in ergonomic chairs. We stand on subways and trains. On average, we are far less active than our grandparents, and compared with our ancient ancestors, we are sloths.[17] For hundreds of thousands of years, our ancestors tracked game across vast swaths of land and harvested food from wild landscapes.[18] Now we travel by car, hunt for our food in grocery stores, and track feeds on social media.

Is comfort making us too comfortable? Being outdoors in less than comfortable conditions asks us to dig deeper into our resources. Nature challenges us, tests us, and teaches us. In our exodus from nature, have we lost touch with our more elemental selves?

There is a risk when we romanticize the past. On this I agree. But I also think there is an equivalent risk when we romanticize the future. Many contend that we are an adaptable species, that we are adjusting to our indoor, urbanized world, and that we will engineer solutions to every problem. In some ways, I hope that they are right, but the question lingers: Is adapting the same as flourishing?

"Have we become duller, chubbier, and more docile versions of our once wild selves?"

We cannot ignore the realities of the world we live in. We are overweight, depressed, stressed out and in the grips of an opioid crisis. American life expectancy is now, for the first time in the modern era, on the decline.[19] These realities cast a deeply worrisome shadow. Is our domestication partly to blame? Have we tamed ourselves into a state of malaise and ill-health?

AWAKEN YOUR INNER BEAR

Be Elemental: A campfire is elemental. A television is not. A hike is elemental. A stair stepper is not. Adopting a more "elemental" approach to living is an actionable way to reengage our sensory system. An elemental approach invites questions that are worth asking: Is a rawer life a richer life? Is slower sometimes better than faster? Is the world as it was given sometimes better than the world as it's been made? Being more elemental isn't a wholesale renunciation of the modern world. You don't need to give up your hot water heater, coffee maker, or toothpaste. You do, however, need to be open to an alternate paradigm—one that elevates and values direct engagement with the natural world. We can all find different entry points: For some, it's rethinking exercise. For others, it's gardening or a more localized approach to living. The variations are endless. The constant, though, is a pattern of living that values quality and tradition over expediency and modernity.

Flex Your Paleolithic Muscle: Throughout most of our evolutionary history, nobody worked out in gyms. Our ancient ancestors walked a lot, ran a bit, and carried stuff if they had to, but they didn't pump any iron. Obvious? Of course it is, but this simple truth is often overlooked. Many physiologists believe that recreating the natural movement of our ancestors is a better method for body wellness—far better than repetitive motions like bench pressing and power squats. What's the takeaway? You don't need to cancel your gym membership, but you might want to rethink your workout regimen, especially if the only workout you know is the one you learned in high school. For starters, sit less, add more organic movement to your workout, and spend more time outside.[21]

We need to recognize the importance of the wild—both within us and around us—as an essential part of the solution. Hundreds of thousands of years of evolution did not sculpt us to be compliant and passive.[20] We are not meant to wither away in cubicles or bathe in the blue glow of screens.

Our domestication, though beneficial in so many ways, goes against our hard-wiring in other ways and too often lulls us into complacency. To tamp down and ignore our wilder inheritance, as we are increasingly doing, is to deny ourselves a bountiful source of strength, betterment, and renewal.

CHAPTER 2

FIND YOUR TRAIL

"To be whole. To be complete. Wildness reminds us what it
means to be human, what we are connected to rather than
what we are separate from."
— *Terry Tempest Williams*

My son sat in protest under a gnarled juniper like an angry Buddha. His knees, red with dust. His helmet, crooked. His bike sat at his side, abandoned like a derelict ship.

He was six-years-old, and he was born in the year of the tiger. He told me he wanted a new bike, not this one. He was hungry, and his knee pads itched. He recounted his complaints to me each time his little bike tipped over or he ran into a rock or he just felt stubborn, which was often. About ten minutes into the ride, his bike chain slipped, and he banged his shin on the pedal. The tiger was annoyed, and he had good reason.

My wife and I had just hauled him a thousand miles from Washington to Utah. We'd woken him up early. We'd kept him up late. I wasn't particularly pleased with his road trip diet—a happy meal in Montana. Some granola bars. Too many fruit snacks. Maybe an apple. Maybe not.

Eight hours into the drive, as we passed through Pocatello, he started to self-destruct as kids invariably do. He became edgy and impatient. He spilled things. He took to repeating everything his older brother said.

And now, only a day later, here I was, dragging my son away from the hard-won comfort of a vacation rental to a dusty trail in the desert. I hadn't asked his opinion, and now I didn't need to—I could read it in his eyes, see it written on his shin.

At six, he still mostly believed that I possessed all the answers in the world. But at that moment, I could tell that he had downgraded my parking lot promise of "so much fun" to "big fat lie."

No one would have blamed me then if I had turned around and headed back to Moab. There was ice cream there and a coffee shop that sold giant chocolate muffins. Our vacation rental was comfortable, the TV enormous, and (though I hadn't admitted it to him yet) I had found out that morning that the swimming pool was most definitely open.

Giving in would have been so easy, so simple. But there was another part of me that saw that bike trail[22] as a battle of wills—the kind of battle that a father needs to win because he's supposed to know that right isn't always easy—sometimes it's fixing a greasy bike chain on a dusty trail in a desert.

Bike rides with six-year-olds are ultimately acts of faith. Rocks and hills and faulty bike components tend to conspire against little wheels and tired legs, yet we still need to believe. We need to believe that kids need bike trails the same way they need home cooking and encouragement and a good night's sleep. Faith isn't easy, but when it's rewarded it can be powerful medicine.

For these reasons, and maybe because I'm a little stubborn too, I pushed on. I fixed his chain. I slapped the dust off his butt. I propped up his spirit with a granola bar, gave him a push, and watched him snake his way across a salmon-colored slab of sandstone.

Eventually, he stopped complaining and we rode together without talking. The breeze had calmed. The sun felt warm on my forearms. The only sound was the click of his bike chain and the occasional cricket chirp of his brake pads. And then, as the trail looped back towards the trailhead, I realized that he had started humming.

"We need to believe that kids need bike trails the same way they need home cooking and encouragement and a good night's sleep."

It may seem like a small thing, his humming, and maybe in some ways it was, but to me it felt infinitely right and true. I'm convinced that when kids feels a hum-inspiring calmness like that, the feeling goes straight into their frontal lobe or heart or spirit or chakra—or wherever it is that truly meaningful experiences go—and it becomes a building block that shores up who they are.

The calm doesn't last, of course. It never does. Along the way kids must learn this too—just as they must learn that journeys aren't always measured in miles, and that the answer to *Are we there yet?* is rarely *yes*.

ANOTHER WAY TO PAY ATTENTION

"Let yourself be silently drawn by the strong pull of what you really love."
—Rumi

Right now, you are reading. You are staring at words arranged in sentences within paragraphs within a book. The words are forming into images in your mind. You are making judgements, decoding, and synthesizing and trying your best to block out distractions and be attentive. And right now, I'm staring at a computer screen and typing. I'm trying my best to stay focused too.

Both writing and reading require something neurologists call "sustained directed attention."[23] Sustained directed attention is what our brain does when we do things like watch TV, scan emails, write, and read. It's an important skill in our modern world, a way of curating the stimuli that enters our brain. But curation comes at cost: It taxes our prefrontal cortex, which eventually causes mental fatigue.

My brain is a little tired. That's what I'm trying to tell you. I'm wishing right now that I could be elsewhere, riding on a bike trail, perhaps. Maybe you feel the same way too.

When we are on a bike trail (or in any pleasant place in nature) something remarkable happens in our brain. A natural environment—its colors, shadows, and smells—

engages our brain differently. The mental workload is dispersed, other zones in the brain light up, and the direct attention machinery slows down or stops completely. Our brain shifts into a mode called "soft fascination."[24] To put it more simply, our brain feels good.

"A natural environment—its colors, shadows, and smells—engages our brain differently."

We all know the feeling. It's the reprieve we get when we watch the sun set or waves roll. It's the calm we feel when we look up at the clouds. In my son's case, it was the hum-inspiring peace he felt when the red sand and junipers finally gave his brain a break.

Soft fascination is easy on the brain. Neurologists call it "involuntary" attention because it's paying attention without effort—when it happens we don't even realize that we are even thinking.[25]

Scientists have known about soft fascination for decades, but until recently it was impossible to quantify with empirical data.

Now, though, research teams can attach mobile electrodes to test subjects and measure brain activity in a variety of environments. The results consistently reveal relaxed states in natural environments and the reverse in urban environments. Bike trails are calming. Crowded streets are not.

And soft fascination isn't just calming. Tapping into soft fascination improves the tools in your cognitive tool box. When your mind shifts into soft fascination, it functions in a way that allows space for reflection, creative thought, and flashes of insight. Einstein walked near the ocean when he needed to solve difficult problems. Now we know why.

AWAKEN YOUR INNER BEAR

Go Hunting for Fractals: A fractal is a complex pattern that repeats itself in finer and finer detail (a snowflake, for instance, or a chambered nautilus). Several recent studies have discovered that even though fractals are complicated, there's something profoundly calming about their repetitive beauty that shifts the brain into a more relaxed gear.[28] The next time you are outside, be more deliberate about studying the landscape that surrounds you. Something as simple as a flock of birds or a riffle in a river might be doing you more good than you realize.

Be an Alpha Predator: Nature can be incredibly restorative, particularly if you immerse yourself in it for more than a single day. Multiple studies have found that alpha waves in the brain are a signature of soft fascination. Recent studies have also found that alpha waves ramp up dramatically by the second or third day of an immersive nature experience.[29] Why is this important? Neuroscientists now know that an increase in alpha brain waves is not only calming, it's also directly linked to reduced depressive symptoms and increased creative thinking.

Neuroscientists are still debating the nuances of soft fascination. Do certain colors activate neurochemicals? Is something happening on a microbial level? Do terpenes released from trees calm us?[26] We may never understand all the mechanisms that trigger soft fascination, but we do know this: The basic recipe usually includes a dose of nature.[27]

The takeaway? Spending time in your backyard is good for you. A walk in a quiet park, even better. An afternoon spent on a social media ... well, you get the idea. Soft fascination often happens by chance, but you can (as any monk or mystic will tell you) be more deliberate about the process. If you can find a natural setting that is rich in scope (textures, colors, etc.), life (birds, fish, etc.), and natural movement (clouds, water, etc.), your chance of shifting into soft fascination increases. The benefits of soft fascination are similar in many ways to the benefits of meditation, but with one key difference: Soft fascination doesn't require the skill or dedication of meditation. Since not everyone inclines towards meditative or yogic practices, soft fascination offers an actionable alternative (no yoga pants required).

MIND LIKE WATER

"Those who are possessed by nothing possess everything."
—Morihei Ueshiba

Have you ever watched a surfer ride a perfect wave, channeling the power of the ocean into unbelievable harmony? This is flow.

If flow had an image, it would be water—fluid, powerful, effortless. If flow had a sound, it would be the soft humming of a happy six-year-old boy.

Flow goes by many names. Taoists call it *Wu Wei*. Athletes call it *The Zone*. A dervish might call it the *Kebal*, the source of all perfection. The most poetic comparison might be what the Japanese call *Mizu no Kokoro*, the "mind like water," a mind so in tune with the universe that it resembles a still pond reflecting a mirror image of its surroundings.

If you've heard about flow (and it's likely that you have), you can thank the psychologist and author Mihaly Csíkszentmihályi (pronounced 'CHICK-sent-me-high-ee'). Csíkszentmihályi is credited with coining the term "flow," and he's written nine books on the subject—many of them best-sellers.

"Flow goes by many names. Taoists call it Wu Wei. Athletes call it The Zone. A dervish might call it the Kebal, the source of all perfection."

For Csíkszentmihályi, our happiness and vitality is dependent on our ability to manifest flow. But what exactly is flow? According to Csíkszentmihályi, flow is a state of mind that arises when we get so wrapped up in an activity that we lose self-awareness and the rest of the world seems to disappear. It's not a daydream or a mind-wander. It's a profoundly calming state of heightened consciousness and effortless focus.

Csíkszentmihályi describes it like this: "The ego falls away. Time flies. Every action, movement, and thought follows inevitably from the previous one, like playing jazz. Your whole being is involved, and you're using your skills to the utmost."[30] Only when we come out of flow do we realize how time has actually passed.

Flow shares some commonalities with soft fascination, and sometimes the two overlap, but they are not the same. The calm of flow arises in moments of extreme focus while the calm of soft fascination is the opposite—it arises in moments when focus is dispersed.

Flow, with the right combination of circumstances, can happen nearly anywhere. You don't need to drive halfway across the country to find it. You don't need special equipment. You can find flow while playing chess, fixing a carburetor, or writing. But outdoor activities (like kayaking on a river, skiing in deep powder, or mountain biking on a desert trail) create a particularly inviting catalyst. Csíkszentmihályi believes it's because of the alchemy of challenge, freedom, and intrinsic enjoyment that often arises in the outdoors.

AWAKEN YOUR INNER BEAR

Slip into Liquid: Water (no surprise) is a well-known and powerful trigger for flow. When in water, the brain relaxes because it has fewer muscular needs and fewer visual and auditory distractions. Water also triggers a mildly meditative state that author and marine biologist Wallace Nichols calls the "blue mind."[31] Also noteworthy: Jeremy Jones, pioneering snowboarder, enjoys a frozen version of "blue mind" that he calls "white moments." The upshot? Bruce Lee was right when he advised: "Become like water, my friend."

Find the Rhythm: Neuroscientists have long known that the synchrony of certain rhythmic sounds, cadences, and repetitive motions can nudge the brain into a state of flow.[32] Paddling, surfing, rock climbing, and fly fishing are only a few of the countless examples of outdoor activities that invite synchrony. Scottish mountaineer and poet Nan Shepherd explains it like this: The rhythm of motion takes us to the still center of our being where the senses are "keyed" and one becomes "not bodiless, but essential body."[33]

Tapping into flow is the holy grail of contentment and calm and the optimal state of consciousness, but you can't just turn flow on. There is no magic switch. Flow is like sleep—the best you can do is to set the stage and create an optimal environment for it to arise.

How? Choose an activity that you find enjoyable and absorbing—preferably one that takes you outside. The magic happens when you strike the right balance between challenge, skill, and pleasure. There's no one way to find flow, and the process is different for all of us. The flow-inducing activity may be skydiving for one person but gardening for another—both are equally valid.

The trick with flow is to find an activity that allows you to focus your psychic energy into a single channel of consciousness. Concentrating on a flow activity allows your mind to enter a remarkable state in which it's simultaneously focused but also joyously relaxed.[34]

Once you choose your flow activity, let yourself settle into its rhythms. Remember, you can't will yourself into flow (and you probably won't even know that you're experiencing flow until it's over). Also remember, flow is dynamic. In other words, as you improve at the activity you may have to increase the intensity to continue to experience the escape of flow—too easy and the mind wanders; too difficult and the mind overthinks the details of the task.

If you tap into flow consistently, you'll feel more capable, confident, and calm. It's mind like water. Effortless perfection. The soft hum of peace and calm.

CHAPTER 3

MORE SOUND, LESS NOISE

"It seemed a shame to stay inside."
—*John Cheever*

A curious garter snake regarded us as we pitched our tent by the lake.[35] The water was calm. Pan-sized trout sipped grasshoppers along the shoreline. It was mid-morning when we arrived. Within an hour, the sun was high above. The water shimmered and insects buzzed in the warmth.

Toby, my ten-year-old son, pulled a book from his backpack, staked his claim on a patch of grass, and began reading. I picked huckleberries with my younger son, Koji, and explored the other end of the lake.

That night by the campfire Toby told me about his book, *Hatchet*—a novel I knew by name but had never read. Here's the gist: A 13-year-old boy survives a plane crash and spends two months alone in the Canadian wilderness. He has an axe, but nothing else. Toby made it sound so interesting that the next morning I sat down on a rock and read it cover-to-cover.

The parallels between *Hatchet* and our camping trip were almost absurdly perfect. In the book, the boy (named Brian, my name too) builds a shelter, finds berries, sparks a fire with his hatchet, and makes a bow and arrow for shooting fish. As I read, my boys caught half a dozen trout (using those feckless grasshoppers as bait). They hoovered huckleberries until their hands were purple. They swam in their underwear. They spent an hour, shirtless and grinning, overturning rocks in search of that suddenly-not-so-curious snake. Not life-and-death survival, exactly, but no less necessary.

Hatchet was published in 1987. Since then, the radius around homes where kids are allowed to roam has shrunk dramatically.[36] It's a fraction of what it was in the '70s when I was a boy. Fewer kids play in parks. Recess play is highly regulated. School playgrounds have been sanitized and mind-numbingly standardized.

You probably don't need to be reminded that our world is changing faster than ever. There's a tangible acceleration, an exponential doubling. More people. More technology. More information. The world, in so many ways, feels louder and faster, like a wave gathering speed as it rolls.

And yet—as I sat there reading on that rock—my wild tribe of two reminded me that all was not lost. They proved that there is still an innate wildness within us.[37] The wave of modernity hasn't swept us under yet, not entirely.

"There is still an innate wildness within us."

Yes, it would be wonderful if the wild came to us unsummoned, but we now live in a world that is increasingly removed from anything truly wild. So we must teach ourselves, actively remind ourselves, what being wild means. We must make room for it and invite it back.

The wild is still within us. I believe that this is true. Spend time with a child in the woods and you will believe it too. But even with children, the wild inside sometimes needs a nudge. A stirring. That's what *Hatchet* reminded me of in so many words, that's what hands purpled by huckleberries symbolize, and that's why fried trout caught with grasshoppers taste so damn good.

FAST TWITCH ANIMALS

"The temple bell stops
But the sound keeps coming
out of the flowers"
—Matsuo Bashō

Two days on the shore of a mountain lake graces a person with a rarified silence. Mountain silence is a reminder, by contrast, of how full of noise the modern world has become. There's the hum of air conditioners, the buzz of lights and appliances. The lawnmowers, leaf blowers, airplanes, and sirens. The door is open—*beep*. The battery is charged—*chirp*. A text message awaits—*ding*.

No noise exists on the shore of a mountain lake, only sound. And sound is different from noise—it's pleasing to the ear like music or the soft babble of a brook. The word "noise" itself is derived from the Latin word for "nausea."

Already in the 1800s, the naturalist John Muir was worried about the too-muchness of our noisy world, calling us "nerve-shaken" and "over-civilized."[38] More recently, author and professor David Gessner has called us "fast twitch" animals, contending that the constant cacophony of vibrations and sounds is like having an alarm clock continually going off in our brains.[39]

"Sound is different from noise—it's pleasing to the ear like music or the soft babble of a brook."

But noise is more than mere distraction. Studies continually show that noise pollution increases systolic blood pressure, hypertension, and hyperactivity.[40] It impairs sleep and reduces our ability to remember and comprehend what we read. Too much noise ramps up our hard-wired "fight or flight" response, which puts our nerves on high alert, which in turn stresses our cardiovascular system. Noise exposure, according to the Washington Post, is becoming "the new second-hand smoke."[41]

Ironically, we sometimes increase the noise to drown out the noise. We replace one noise with another or plug our ears with ear buds and noise-canceling headphones. It's a practice particularly popular with our youth, birthing an entire generation that will spend a fair share of their formative years living in little bubbles of auditory solitude—a strange phenomenon that may, incidentally, add tinnitus, loneliness, and diminished social skills to the long list of the downstream consequences of man-made noise.

The disruptions of man-made noise aren't anything new. In 1787, the founding fathers—needing peace and quiet to scratch out a constitution—ordered trailer-loads of dirt spread on the cobblestone around Independence Hall.[42] They needed to muffle the clatter of horse hooves so they could do some thinking. In ancient Rome, chariot traffic was forbidden at night because it disrupted sleep.[43]

The Romans and America's founding fathers, for all their foresight, had no way a fathoming the ruckus that we now endure. Our horses and chariots never cease. On some days, the noise in Midtown Manhattan can hit 95 decibels—that's the equivalent noise of a subway train from 200 feet.[44]

Distraction defines us. We are beset by noise. But it wasn't always this way. Our hearing circuitry evolved in a decidedly quieter world. For hundreds of thousands of years, the soundscape was one of birdsong and insect. Wind and rain. Thunder and waterfall. It wasn't an easy world, no doubt. There was hardship and disease. Food was sometimes scarce and often tasteless. Predators were large and omnipresent. Danger lurked. No, the steppes and savannas probably weren't as idyllic as many (myself included) are wont to believe, but whatever the wild past may have been, we can be certain of one thing—it was quite likely the last time we could truly hear ourselves think.

AWAKEN YOUR INNER BEAR

Choose Quieter Ways: We can choose to move in more silent ways—like walking, bicycling, and cross country skiing; we can choose to engage more frequently in silent pursuits—like backpacking, gardening, and rock climbing; we can choose to seek out more silent places—like rivers, trails, and remote beaches; we can also choose to gift silence to our children by encouraging unplugged and outdoor play.

Seek the Sound of Silence: Where's the quietest place in the lower forty-eight? Most estimates place it in Washington State at N 48.12885°- W 123.68234° in a mossy grove of trees in the Hoh Rain Forest. The exact spot, which is nicknamed One Square Inch of Silence, is marked by a small red stone on top of a moss-covered tree.[45] Obviously, we can't all rush to the Hoh, but we can each seek out our own pockets of quiet solitude. Extended immersion in a silent environment has been shown to reduce stress. It also creates new brain cells in the brain region linked to learning and recall.

We can't merely look back with gauzy eyes and wish that life were quieter, nor is it enough to say, yes, that is how it once was but is no more—we need to give silence explicit value.

There is no one perfect silence, but places with nourishing silences tend to share three commonalities: Limited auditory noise, no technology, and a softening of visual input. These three silences, in turn, create a pocket of inner space free from the incessant chatter of modern life.

ABORIGINAL SENSIBLE MUCHNESS

"There is nothing in the intelligence which did not first
pass through the senses."
—Aristotle

When I was a boy, it was a badge of honor to come home with purple fingers and a bucket of huckleberries—a sure guarantee of pie for dessert or pancakes for breakfast. It meant I'd spent the day in the mountains. A good day. A day filled with the smell of bear grass and pine and the chattering of chipmunks in the shadowed woods.

Finding a bush loaded with berries was like finding a treasure. The act itself felt ancient, like I was in the present and simultaneous 5,000 years old.[46] Simple as it is, I can think of few activities more immersive and sensory rich than collecting huckleberries.

When picking huckleberries you feel, taste, smell, see, and listen your way through the woods. You balance, orient, and scan. All the while your brain is lit up like a pinball machine, and neural pathways are strengthened and formed as you synthesize and remember the sensory input. Our ability to process this array of sensory input is part of what makes us human.

Our senses are meant to collaborate, not to fly solo or toil in lonely pairs. We are calibrated to process information through touch, taste, smell, sight, and hearing as well as other less obvious sensory tools like balance and reflex. A richer sensory experience is, on a very basic level, a richer life.

"Our senses are meant to collaborate, not to fly solo or toil in lonely pairs."

Food, for instance, is more pleasurable when multiple senses are engaged. Think about the smell of coffee, the bouquet of wine, and the tartness of a huckleberry. Food at its best is a multi-modal sensory experience.

Over time, a rich sensory experience also allows us to be more alert, mindful, and safe. A firefighter smells fire, listens for fire, feels fire. We jokingly say our mothers have "eyes on the back of their heads," but the joke is anchored in truth—mothers, particularly new mothers, are remarkably attuned to sensory signals.

Our brains need huckleberry picking, or its sensory equivalent, the way our bodies need nourishment. Yet, more and more, that's not always what we give them.

Ancient hunters, foragers, farmers (and even our grandparents) all employed a vastly different sensory toolkit than we employ today. *Which way is north? Will it rain tonight? What's the quickest way home?* Answering these questions once required experience and synthesis. Today we arrive at the same answers in a fraction of the time without leaving our couches. Are we more accurate and more efficient? Yes, and maybe yes again. But all of it begs the question: What happens to the human mind when its primary input arrives via binary code and electroluminescent screens? What happens when virtual reality becomes a surrogate for actual experience?

In a now famous study, cab drivers who memorized London's labyrinth of streets were found to have a significantly larger hippocampus (the region of the brain that specializes in memory) than cab drivers who relied on a GPS.[47] In other words, when they stopped using their sensory toolkit to create a mental map of London, they began losing mental horsepower.

A GPS, for all its remarkable capabilities, leaves no lasting impression and no memories. Like most technology, a GPS delivers meaning through only two channels—sight and sound. It's virtual, not real. Secondary, not primary. Synthetic, not actual.

If we depend too much on technologies like the GPS, we become passive receptors and to a certain degree, even helpless. We become followers rather than thinkers, tourists rather than explorers. We don't engage our sensory toolkit in a way that forms rich memories, builds knowledge, or fully activates the plasticity of our brains.

Our technology makes our lives easy. True. But ease is often a double-edged sword. We hardly move a muscle to use technology. We take it in from our homes and cars and offices. We are bombarded with stimuli and swollen with information but too often bereft of sensory experience. There's no dirt under the nails. There's no smell. There's no smooth patina or rough edge. There are no stains on the fingers.

"What happens to the human mind when its primary input arrives via binary code and electroluminescent screens? What happens when virtual reality becomes a surrogate for actual experience?"

What's the quickest way home? What's the weather? Just ask Siri or Alexa. We have willingly given up a rich sensory skillset because in the bargain we have gained a bevy of technological shortcuts and conveniences. Why, we tell ourselves, should information come with dirt or smell or a touch of discomfort? Why fight the cobwebs and dust of musty tombs? Why pick huckleberries when we can order them online and have them delivered next-day air? This, anyway, is the conventional argument.

Such thinking arises from the same question—the same "why?"—that my students always asked when I made them read printed books rather than digital versions. I wanted them to touch and smell the text, dog-ear the pages, doodle and color between the lines. I told them these things matter, that the brain prefers a five-course meal, not a protein shake—a Jackson Pollock, not a paint-by-number.

As infants, we were all intensely attuned to our sensory experience. None of us remember it, but it was a large part of what made us who we are today. A baby's world is awash in colors, tastes, and sounds—what the psychologist William James poetically called an "aboriginal sensible muchness."[48] As we mature, however, we learn to edit the input. Editing is a natural and necessary part of our development. The problem, though, is that our modern world invites *over* editing. Our "aboriginal sensible muchness" is starved when restricted to a drip-feed diet of googled answers and light-emitting diodes.

When it comes to babies, we all seem to agree that there's a relationship between sensory experience and cognitive development. It's why we paint a baby's room, buy colorful toys, and play music to the baby as it nestles in the womb. Yet we adults rarely give ourselves the same suite of experiences. We preach one sermon but practice another.

AWAKEN YOUR INNER BEAR

Find the Balance: Since balance isn't one of the five classic senses that was drilled into our heads when we were kids, it's easy to forget that it's part of our sensory toolkit. But it is. Balance is a combination of our vestibular sense (our ears' ability to feel rotation, gravity, and movement) and our proprioception sense (our awareness of our body's position in space). Balance, like most of our senses, slowly diminishes with age. Staying active slows the process. Staying active in the outdoors slows it even more. The uneven surfaces in nature fire up the small stabilizing muscles that remain inactive when we are sitting (or even when doing many conventional gym workouts) and give our sense of balance an amazing workout.

Be Hands on: According to neurologist and author Frank Wilson, the hand is the focal point of our ability to create and discover.[49] Wilson believes that in addition to allowing us to throw stones and spears, our hands laid the groundwork for our sizable intelligence. A "hands on" educational philosophy allows us to feel our way to answers and encourages imagination in ways that a "hands off" education does not. What does this mean in practical terms? Less learning via screens and more learning via real-world experiences.

Wake up and Smell the Coffee: Intentionally smelling powerful scents (like ground coffee or mint leaves) engages receptors in your nose. While it may sound trivial, it's not. Doctors call it "scent therapy" and it works.[50] You can improve your sense of smell over time if you work at it. Since smell is closely linked to attraction, safety, and memory, exercising your sense of smell is a good idea. One great way to fire up your senses is to move your nose closer to the natural landscape. Give mushroom foraging, berry picking, or spelunking a try.

How often do we step outside with the sole intent of smelling the rain or feeling the breeze? How often do we intentionally nourish our minds with a richer diet of sensory experience? Or more pointedly, how many hours do we stare at screens and sit in cars and offices? We know exercise is good for our bodies, so we join gyms and slog away on Stairmaster machines. We know diet is good for our health, so we watch (or try to watch) what we eat. Our sensory systems need the same attention.

We must reconsider the measure of how we engage in the world around us and why it's important. Fewer smart phones. More campfires. Fewer tweets. More starry nights. Fewer commutes. More walks. Fewer downloads. More huckleberries. Activating our full sensory toolkit is exercise and nourishment for our brains.

THE BEAR AWAKENS

*"To use the world well, to be able to stop wasting it and
our time in it, we need to relearn our being in it."*
—*Ursula K. Le Guin*

In 1807, Thomas Jefferson received a pair of grizzly bears cubs as a gift from the explorer Captain Zebulon Pike. Pike purchased the cubs, one male and one female, somewhere along the Continental Divide.[51]

Pike knew little of bears, particularly grizzly bears, and Jefferson probably knew less, but Jefferson couldn't resist owning what Pike described as "the most ferocious animals of the continent."[52] It didn't go well. The bears were caged on the White House lawn for a while, then moved to a museum in Philadelphia. The story goes downhill from there. Shortly after arriving in Philadelphia, one of the bears escaped its cage, terrorized the museum, and was finally shot dead. The second bear was quickly put down as well.[53]

Today we know that grizzly bears are difficult to keep in captivity. A bear's nature is to roam free over a range of hundreds of miles. Confine a grizzly to a small space and it paces and denudes its teeth on the bars. Bears can adapt to captivity in the sense that they can "live" in captivity, but the real question is not whether they can *live* but whether they can *flourish.*[54]

This is our question too. Look around. How many of us are, in a way, like Jefferson's grizzlies? Our cubicles, our feeds, our routines, our commutes—aren't they all just bars in a cell? Is there a rawer, wilder self deep within us longing to break out? Don't we, like the bear, need open spaces? Don't we, like the bear, need to roam free? Reconnecting with our wilder natures—waking up, you might say, our inner bear—is a crucial component in our well-being.

Buddhists say there are 84,000 paths to enlightenment. We each awaken our inner bear, it seems to me, in a similar way—on our own unique path. For each of us, the relationship with the wild is necessarily different. For some, it is a new acquaintance. For others, a return. For still others, a continuation and a broadening.

There are forces everywhere conspiring against our potential and our contentment, but we must not underestimate our ability to change. Change is not easy, but it's not impossible. Becoming different people is something that humans do when we choose to wrestle with deep problems.[55]

There will be nine billion people on the planet soon. Despite our politicians' saber rattling and myopic bumbling, I don't think we're going anywhere soon, which brings me to a crucial point: Our well-being depends on our willingness to radically rethink how we imagine our relationship with the wild. Rather than lord over nature or mourn the end of nature as we know it, we need to think about the kind of nature we want, both now and in the future, and seek it out. At the same time, we need to think about the wild within us, our inherited wildness of being. We are the recipients of a remarkable evolutionary legacy that needs to be mindfully curated.

"Our well-being depends on our willingness to radically rethink how we imagine our relationship with the wild."

In closing, I'd like to wish you a life of adventure, a life filled with starry nights, loyal dogs, campfires, and bike rides that make you hum. I hope you find fascination in the woods, calm in the mountains, and that your hands are soon purpled by a bounty of huckleberries.

The end goal, for all of us, should be to approach life with excitement and zest, to feel alive and activated, and to live a life that is wild and authentic. But none of this happens on its own. There are levers that we need to pull, and we need to ask the right questions: *Why and where are we meant to roam? What animates us? What challenges us? What sustains us?* Then we need to pursue the answers and awaken the bear within.

WORKS CITED, COMMENTARY, AND READING SUGGESTIONS

THE BEAR STIRS

"Time collapsed as I locked eyes with that bear. My mind went quiet": The ecologist Paul Shepard writes extensively (and often brilliantly) about interacting and connecting with the non-human world. Shepard begins in the Paleolithic. From his perspective "the human species emerged enacting, dreaming, and thinking animals." The animal world (or "The Other," to use his expression) is an essential component in our ecological community and part of our primal heritage. Shepard is more committed to the Paleolithic perspective than I am, but his insights continues to shape my thinking. I highly recommend exploring his work, starting with *The Others: How Animals Made Us Human.*

WILD AS THE WIND

[2] Manito Park, the park that I am referencing in this essay, was designed by Frederick Law Olmsted who also designed Central Park. He describes an ideal outdoor space this way: "The enjoyment of scenery employs the mind without fatigue and yet exercises it; tranquilizes it and yet enlivens it; and thus, through the influence of the mind over the body gives the effect of refreshing rest and reinvigoration to the whole system." For further reading on Olmsted and our relationship with nature, I suggest Florence Williams *The Nature Fix: Why Nature Makes Us Happier, Healthier, and More Creative.*

[3] My image of bio-centrism resembles another image that I have seen on a variety of websites. In some of its appearances the image is associated with Johanna Grabow. I haven't yet confirmed the source of the original, but I offer this footnote as an acknowledgement and a thank you to the person who first conceived the idea, Johanna or otherwise.

[4] *"The story of our wilder selves still echoes in our subconscious like the whisper of a ghost."*: Psychologist Gordon H. Orians believes that our latent hunger for nature manifests in what he calls "ghosts"—evolutionary remnants of our past which are hard-wired into our nervous system. For more on this idea, I suggest Orians' *Snakes, Sunrises, and Shakespeare: How Evolution Shapes Our Loves and Fears.*

[5] *"Hunting and fishing licenses ... and other indicators of nature recreation have been steady waning."*: Pergams, O. R. W., and P. A. Zaradic. "Evidence for a Fundamental and Pervasive Shift Away from Nature-Based Recreation." *Proceedings of the National Academy of Sciences,* vol. 105, no. 7, 2008, pp. 2295–2300., doi:10.1073/pnas.0709893105.

[6] *"...national park attendance ... has been steadily waning."*: Stevens, Thomas H., et al. "Declining National Park Visitation." *Journal of Leisure Research,* vol. 46, no. 2, 2014, pp. 153–164., doi:10.1080/00222216.2014.11950317.

[7] *"American adults spend over ninety percent of their lives inside vehicles or buildings"*: Klepeis, Neil E, et al. "The National Human Activity Pattern Survey (NHAPS): a Resource for Assessing Exposure to Environmental Pollutants." *Journal of Exposure Science & Environmental Epidemiology,* vol. 11, no. 3, 2001, pp. 231–252., doi:10.1038/sj.jea.7500165: https://www.nature.com/articles/7500165, accessed January 8, 2019.

[8] *"The average American teen spends nine hours a day online.":* Tsukayama, Hayley. "Teens Spend Nearly Nine Hours Every Day Consuming Media." *The Washington Post,* WP Company, 3 Nov. 2015, www.washingtonpost.com/news/the-switch/wp/2015/11/03/teens-spend-nearly-nine-hours-every-day-consuming-media/

[9] *"We live now in in what writer Richard Louv calls "protective house arrest.":* Louv, Richard. *Last Child in the Woods. Algonquin Books Od Chapel Hill, 2006.*

[10] *"Studies continually confirm that the microbiota that we encounter in nature is beneficial.":* Thompson, Helen. "Early Exposure to Germs Has Lasting Benefits." *Nature,* 2012, doi:10.1038/nature.2012.10294.

[11] *"Dog owners have fewer heart attacks.":* Levine, Glenn N., et al. "Pet Ownership and Cardiovascular Risk." *Circulation,* vol. 127, no. 23, 2013, pp. 2353–2363., doi:10.1161/cir.0b013e31829201e1.

[12] *"Petting a dog boosts our immune system…":* Charnetski, Carl J., et al. "Effect of Petting a Dog on Immune System Function." *Psychological Reports,* vol. 95, no. 3_suppl, 2004, pp. 1087–1091., doi:10.2466/pr0.95.3f.1087-1091.

[13] *"Petting a dog … reduces stress hormones.":* Petersson, Maria, et al. "Oxytocin and Cortisol Levels in Dog Owners and Their Dogs Are Associated with Behavioral   Patterns: An Exploratory Study." *Frontiers in Psychology,* vol. 8, 2017, doi:10.3389/fpsyg.2017.01796.

THE TAMING OF THE YOU

[14] My thinking on the "domestication" of our species is informed primarily by the "Neural Crest Cell Hypothesis" developed by Richard Wrangham of Harvard, Adam Wilkins, now at Humboldt University in Germany, and Tecumseh Fitch at the University of Vienna, Austria.

[15] Jared Diamond famously and controversially described the agricultural revolution as "The worst mistake in the history of the human race." Diamond's viewpoint, from my perspective, is weakened at times by speculative leaps and causal reduction, but I still highly recommend exploring his work, starting with *Guns, Germs, and Steel.*

[16] *"...studies suggest that too much time indoors plays havoc with are circadian rhythms, which in turn fuels insomnia and anxiety."*: Duffy, Jeanne F., and Charles A. Czeisler. "Effect of Light on Human Circadian Physiology." *Sleep Medicine Clinics,* vol. 4, no. 2, 2009, pp. 165–177., doi:10.1016/j.jsmc.2009.01.004.

[17] *"On average, we are far less active than our grandparents, and compared with our ancient ancestors, we are sloths."*: Hill, J. O. "Obesity and the Environment: Where Do We Go from Here?" *Science,* vol. 299, no. 5608, 2003, pp. 853–855., doi:10.1126/science.1079857.

[18] *"... our ancestors tracked game across vast swaths of land..."*: Many evolutionary psychologists speak of how our "stone age minds" are trapped in our modern bodies. I find this point of view interesting but not entirely reasonable. I'm of the opinion that our bodies and minds are the ongoing product of evolution, a complex combination of adaptations that are both recent and ancient. A number of current studies have demonstrated that selection can dramatically alter the traits of a population in as few as 18-20 generations (for humans, that's roughly 400-500 years). So to say that we still have "stone age minds" isn't entirely accurate. Do elements of our primitive selves remain within us? Absolutely. All of this informs my opinion when I speak about our ancient ancestors. For further reading on this subject, I suggest *Paleofantasy: What Evolution Really Tells Us About Sex, Diet, and How We Live* by Marlene Zuk, and *The Story of the Human Body: Evolution, Health and Disease* by Daniel Lieberman.

[19] *"American life expectancy is now, for the first time in the modern era, on the decline."*: Bernstein, Lenny. "U.S. Life Expectancy Declines Again, a Dismal Trend Not Seen since World War I." *The Washington Post,* WP Company, 29 Nov. 2018, www.washingtonpost.com/national/health-science/us-life-expectancy-declines-again-a-dismal-trend-not-seen-since-world-war-i/2018/11/28/ae58bc8c-f28c-11e8-bc79-68604ed88993_story.html accessed December 23, 2018.

[20] For three very different perspectives on our tribal past, I recommend *Tribe: On Homecoming and Belonging* by Sebastian Junger, *Where We Belong: Beyond Abstraction in Perceiving Nature* by Paul Shepard, and *Catching Fire: How Cooking Made Us Human* by Richard Wrangham.

[21] *"Flex Your Paleolithic Muscles"*: For more on organic exercise, I suggest the following resource: http://www.greenexercise.org

FIND YOUR TRAIL

[22] The trail Koji and I rode that day was the Lazy-EZ loop in the Moab Brand Trail network. It's a perfect ride for newbies or anyone unfamiliar with desert single track. The scenery is stunning, there are lots of trail options, and it's close to town. Cool Fact: The names of the main Brand Trails are based on cattle brands and spell out M-o-a-b. Bar <u>M</u>, Circle <u>O</u>, Rockin <u>A</u>, Bar <u>B</u>. One more thing: If you do go to Moab, pack a copy of Edward Abbey's *Desert Solitaire.*

ANOTHER WAY TO PAY ATTENTION

[23] *"Both writing and reading require something neurologists call 'sustained directed attention'"*: Berman, Marc G. "The Restorative Benefits of Interacting with Nature: Cognitive and Neuroscientific Perspectives." *PsycEXTRA Dataset,* 2014, doi:10.1037/e533002014-001.For a deeper dive into this idea, I recommend reading *The Experience of Nature: A Psychological Perspective* by Rachel and Steven Kaplan

[24] *"Our brain shifts into a mode called 'soft fascination'"*: Berman, Marc G. "The Restorative Benefits of Interacting with Nature: Cognitive and Neuroscientific Perspectives." *PsycEXTRA Dataset*, 2014, doi:10.1037/e533002014-001.

[25] *"...when it happens don't even realize that we are even thinking"*: Kaplan, Stephen. "The Restorative Benefits of Nature: Toward an Integrative Framework." *Journal of Environmental Psychology*, vol. 15, no. 3, 1995, pp. 169–182., doi:10.1016/0272-4944(95)90001-2.

[26] *"Do terpenes released from trees calm us?"*: There are several ongoing studies in Japan and Korea exploring this possibility. This study is an excellent starting point: Cho, Kyoung Sang, et al. "Terpenes from Forests and Human Health." *Toxicological Research*, vol. 33, no. 2, 2017, pp. 97–106., doi:10.5487/tr.2017.33.2.097: https://www.ncbi.nlm.nih.gov/pmc/articles/PMC5402865/, accessed Jan 5, 2019.

[27] *"...The basic recipe usually includes a dose of nature"*: Kaplan, Stephen. "The Restorative Benefits of Nature: Toward an Integrative Framework." *Journal of Environmental Psychology*, vol. 15, no. 3, 1995, pp. 169–182., doi:10.1016/0272-4944(95)90001-2.

[28] *"...there's something profoundly calming about their repetitive beauty that shifts the brain into a more relaxed gear"*: Marcheschi, C. Boydston, and R. P. Taylor, "Human Physiological Benefits of Viewing Nature: EEG Responses to Exact and Statistical Fractal Patterns." *Nonlinear Dynamics, Psychology, and Life Sciences*, Vol. 19, No. 1, pp. 1-12. © 2015 Society for Chaos Theory in Psychology & Life Sciences. University of Oregon, Eugene, OR. https://cpb-us-e1.wpmucdn.com/blogs.uoregon.edu/dist/e/12535/files/2015/12/art1901-1LITE-13psjqc.pdf, accessed January 17, 2019.

[29] *"...alpha waves in the brain ramp up dramatically by the second or third day of an immersive nature experience"*: Atchley, Ruth Ann, et al. "Creativity in the Wild: Improving

Creative Reasoning through Immersion in Natural Settings."
PLoS ONE, vol. 7, no. 12, 2012,
doi:10.1371/journal.pone.0051474:
https://journals.plos.org/plosone/article?id=10.1371/journal.p
one.0051474, accessed January 8, 2019.

MIND LIKE WATER

[30] Geirland, John. "Go With The Flow." *Wired* magazine,
September, Issue 4.09, 1996.
https://www.wired.com/1996/09/czik/, accessed January 10,
2019.

*[31] Nichols, Wallace J., and Celine Cousteau. Blue Mind: the
Surprising Science That Shows How Being near, in, on, or
under Water Can Make You Happier, Healthier, More
Connected and Better at What You Do. Back Bay Books,
Little, Brown and Company, 2015.*

[32] Alan C. MacPherson, Dave Collins & Sukhvinder S. Obhi
(2009) The Importance of Temporal Structure and Rhythm
for the Optimum Performance of Motor Skills: A New Focus
for Practitioners of Sport Psychology, Journal of Applied
Sport Psychology, 21:sup1, S48-S61, DOI:
10.1080/10413200802595930, accessed January 20, 2019.

[33] Shepherd's poetic description is worth quoting in its
entirety: "Walking thus, hour after hour, the senses keyed,
one walks the flesh transparent. But no metaphor, transparent,
or light as air, is adequate. The body is not made negligible,
but paramount. Flesh is not annihilated but fulfilled. One is
not bodiless, but essential body... It is therefore when the
body is keyed to its highest potential and controlled to a
profound harmony deepening into something that resembles
trance, that I discover most nearly what it is to be.":
Shepherd, Nan, and Robert Macfarlane. *The Living Mountain
a Celebration of the Cairngorm Mountains of Scotland.*
Canongate, 2011.

[34] *"... a remarkable state in which it [the mind] is simultaneously focused but also joyously relaxed."*: Csikszentmihalyi describes it as a "joyous, self-forgetful involvement" that arises through concentration: Csikszentmihalyi, Mihaly (1990). *Flow: The Psychology of Optimal Experience.* New York, NY: Harper and Row.

MORE SOUND, LESS NOISE

[35] For this trip, the boys and I hiked to Roman Nose Lake in Idaho's Selkirk Mountains.

[36] *"...the radius around homes where kids are allowed to roam has shrunk dramatically"*: Numerous studies have attempted to quantify the change. The following study, for example, posits that the independent mobility of children has shrunk by as much as ninety percent over the last fifty years: http://www.psi.org.uk/docs/7350_PSI_Report_CIM_final.pdf

[37] Any mention of our "innate" connection with nature is an implicit reference to E.O. Wilson and his seminal book, *Biophilia: The Human Bond with other Species.*

FAST TWITCH ANIMALS

[38] *"nerve-shaken"* and *"over-civilized"*: Muir, John. *Our National Parks.* The Riverside Press, Cambridge, 1901, 1.

[39] *"... author David Gessner has called us "fast twitch" animals ..."*: Foglia, Lucas and Florence Williams, directors. National Geographic. National Geographic, National Geographic, 25 July 2017, www.nationalgeographic.com/magazine/2016/01/call-to-wild/, accessed December 19, 2018. I also recommend the following book by David Gessner: All the Wild That Remains: Edward Abbey, Wallace Stegner and the American West.

[40] *"Studies continually show that noise pollution increases systolic blood pressure, hypertension, and hyperactivity":* For more on noise pollution I suggest the following study: Hammer, Monica S., et al. "Environmental Noise Pollution in the United States: Developing an Effective Public Health Response." *Environmental Health Perspectives,* vol. 122, no. 2, 2014, pp. 115–119., doi:10.1289/ehp.1307272:https://ehp.niehs.nih.gov/doi/full/1 0.1289/ehp.1307272, accessed January 8, 2019.

[41] *Noise exposure, according to the Washington Post, is becoming "the new second-hand smoke":* Fetterman, Mindy. "Noise Exposure Is Becoming 'the New Secondhand Smoke'." *The Washington Post,* WP Company, 12 May 2018, www.washingtonpost.com/national/health-science/noise-exposure-is-becoming-the-new-secondhand-smoke/2018/05/11/dd080c30-52d3-11e8-9c91-7dab596e8252_story.html, accessed January 18, 2019.

[42] *"In 1787, the founding fathers—needing peace and quiet to scratch out a constitution—ordered trailer-loads of dirt spread on the cobblestone around Independence Hall.":* Goines, Lisa, and Louis Hagler. "Noise Pollution: A Modern Plague." *Southern Medical Journal, vol. 100, no. 3, 2007,* p. 287–294., doi:10.1097/smj.0b013e3180318be5: http://www.nonoise.org/library/smj/smj.htm, accessed January 12, 2019.

[43] *"In ancient Rome, chariot traffic was forbidden at night because it disrupted sleep.":* Ibid.

[44] *"On some days, the noise in Midtown Manhattan can hit 95 decibels…":* Fetterman, Mindy. "Noise Exposure Is Becoming 'the New Secondhand Smoke'." The Washington Post, WP Company, 12 May 2018, www.washingtonpost.com/national/health-science/noise-exposure-is-becoming-the-new-secondhand-smoke/2018/05/11/dd080c30-52d3-11e8-9c91-7dab596e8252_story.html, accessed January 18, 2019.

⁴⁵ Finding a reprieve from noise is difficult, but not impossible. The National Park Service has published a set of "sound maps" that will show you where to escape man made noise. You can find them here: https://www.nps.gov

ABORIGINAL SENSE OF MUCHNESS

⁴⁶ *"The act itself felt ancient, like I was in the present and simultaneous 5,000 years old"*: My phrasing here owes a tip of the hat to Jim Harrison, who put it this way: "When I'm fishing and hunting with the right attitude, I reenter the woods and river with a moment-by-moment sense of the glories of creation, of the natural world as a living fabric of existence, so that I'm both young again but also 70,000 years old" (*Field & Stream*, 2003).

⁴⁷ *"...cab drivers who memorized London's labyrinth of streets were found to have a significantly larger hippocampus than cab drivers who relied on a GPS.": Woollett, Katherine, et al. "Talent in the Taxi: A Model System for Exploring Expertise." Philosophical Transactions of the Royal Society B: Biological Sciences, vol. 364, no. 1522, 2009, pp. 1407–1416., doi:10.1098/rstb.2008.0288.*

⁴⁸ *"aboriginal sensible muchness": James, William. Some Problems of Philosophy. Nabu Press, 2014.*

⁴⁹ *Wilson, Frank R. The Hand: How Its Use Shapes the Brain, Language, and Human Culture. Vintage Books, 1999.*

⁵⁰ *"You can improve your sense of smell over time if you work at it.":* Negoias, Simona & Pietsch, K & Hummel, Thomas. (2016). Changes in Olfactory Bulb Volume Following Lateralized Olfactory Training. Brain Imaging and Behavior. 11. 10.1007/s11682-016-9567-9.

[51] *"Pike purchased the cubs, one male and one female, somewhere along the Continental Divide.":* Pike to Jefferson, October 29, 1807. Transcription available at Founders Online.

[52] *"...the most ferocious animals of the continent.":* Ibid.

[53] *"The second bear was quickly put down as well.":* Gaye Wilson, 2008. "A Wild Gift from the West: Two Grizzly Cubs," in *Monticello Newsletter* 19 (Spring 2008).

[54] *"Bears can adapt to captivity in the sense that they can 'live' in captivity...":* My thinking here as well as my phrasing is inspired by Peter H. Kahn, Jr.'s essay "Environmental Generational Amnesia." The essay can be found in the following collection: Fleischner, Thomas Lowe. *Nature Love Medicine: Essays on Wildness and Wellness.* Torrey House Press, 2017.

[55] *"Becoming different people is something that humans do when we choose to wrestle with deep problems.":* My thinking here as well as my phrasing is inspired by Jedediah Purdy's book *After Nature: A Politics for the Anthropocene.*

Made in the USA
Las Vegas, NV
11 December 2024

13890652R10036